YOUR KNOWLEDGE HAS VALUE

- We will publish your bachelor's and master's thesis, essays and papers

- Your own eBook and book - sold worldwide in all relevant shops

- Earn money with each sale

Upload your text at www.GRIN.com and publish for free

Thomas Hoffmann

Methods for data management and data privacy. Private data aggregation

GRIN Publishing

Bibliographic information published by the German National Library:

The German National Library lists this publication in the National Bibliography; detailed bibliographic data are available on the Internet at http://dnb.dnb.de .

Imprint:

Copyright © 2014 GRIN Verlag GmbH
Print and binding: Books on Demand GmbH, Norderstedt Germany
ISBN: 978-3-656-84258-3

This book at GRIN:

http://www.grin.com/en/e-book/283874/methods-for-data-management-and-data-privacy-private-data-aggregation

GRIN - Your knowledge has value

Since its foundation in 1998, GRIN has specialized in publishing academic texts by students, college teachers and other academics as e-book and printed book. The website www.grin.com is an ideal platform for presenting term papers, final papers, scientific essays, dissertations and specialist books.

Visit us on the internet:

http://www.grin.com/

http://www.facebook.com/grincom

http://www.twitter.com/grin_com

Thomas Hoffmann

Methods for data management and data privacy in the smart grid: Private data aggregation

---

Table of Contents

1   Introduction

Following the nuclear disaster in Fukushima in 2011, the German federal government has decided to shut down half of the existing nuclear power plants in Germany immediately and to not have any nuclear power plants at all running by 2022. To compensate the loss of energy, formerly produced by these power plants, many solar collectors, windmills and other sources of renewable energy are being installed. So instead of having a few big power plants, delivering a predictable amount of energy at all time, the situation will soon be a decentralized grid of less powerful energy sources whose production is dependent on the weather. Also, many of those solar collectors are owned by the general public and are not under the direct control of any big utility company.

1.1   Smart meters

To make this change to renewable energy possible, conventional electric meters need to be replaced with so called "smart meters". A smart meter allows the energy provider to gain a finer granular view of the power consumption in a specific region at a given time. Such information is necessary to manage the many different electricity producers and thereby guarantee a constant supply voltage.

1.2   Privacy risks

On the other hand, obtaining detailed information about the power consumption of a household poses a serious privacy risk for the corresponding residents: [9] has shown that it is possible to determine the movie shown on a LCD TV, solely by analysing the overall power consumption given by a smart meter. Therefore, sending the actual power consumption of a certain household in short intervals to the utility provider should be avoided.

1.3   Private data aggregation

Slightly based on [5], this work will show some protocols to aggregate energy consumption data from multiple smart meters. The aggregation will hide the individual consumption of a single household while still revealing the necessary total consumption of a regional limited area to the utility provider. This way, the electrical supply company still gets the needed information about the demand in an area and can take necessary steps to ensure the supply. On the other hand, the power consumption of all of the participating households is indistinguishable from each other and thereby protects their privacy. As people already submit their power consumption measurement data once or twice a year for billing purposes, we do not assume any privacy issues by aggregating the data of a single household over such a long time. Therefore, we will focus on geographical aggregation of smart meters which submit their measurement in short intervals.

1.4   Adversary model

The aggregated data of several households can not be used for billing purposes as each household should still be billed individually. Therefore, the motivation to manipulate a smart meter or to not correctly participate in an aggregation protocol is small as no one would gain any financial advantage in doing so. However, we consider the utility provider as well as each smart meter to be curious about the consumption of other individual smart meters. Some of the presented protocols even allow to have a small group of malicious or collaborating smart meters, but most of them assume just an *honest-but-curious* adversary model.

2   Smart meter requirements

In Germany, every new build house has to be equipped with a smart meter already. According to §21d I Energiewirtschaftsgesetz (EnWG), all a device has to do to be called a "smart meter" is to show the actual power consumption and to be integrated in some sort of communication network. For most of the presented protocols, these requirements are not enough and additional assumptions about the used smart meters are made, as shown in the following section.

2.1   Cryptographic operations

First of all, the smart meters have to be able to run different kind of cryptographic operations, like encrypting data or digitally sign outgoing packets. Some of these operations, like the use of an asymmetric and partial homomorphic encryption schemes, require quite a lot of computing power, especially if no special hardware chips are build in the smart meter and the operations have to be executed entirely in software.

2.2   Peer-to-Peer communication

Some of the proposed protocols need to establish a data connection with other nearby smart meters. As we don't want to rely on the utility company to provide such information, the meters need be able to discover other smart meters in their neighbourhood on their own. In some papers, a wireless communication module like WiFi, Bluetooth or ZigBee is assumed to be build in the smart meter to establish these peer-to-peer connections.

2.3   Digital certificates

Especially if the smart meters communicate with each other, some way to ensure the integrity and authenticity of the connection has to be found. In general, digital certificates which contain a public encryption key and some kind of identification are used for that. To verify another certificate, each smart meter has to trust a certification authority (CA), which has signed the certificates of the other smart meters. The CA can for example be a governmental institution and its public key has to be preloaded on each smart meter by the manufacturer.

3   Components for privacy-preserving data aggregation

Instead of listing some existing aggregation protocols, this section presents some common cryptographic primitives which might be helpful to design such a protocol. Most of the proposed protocols for privacy-aware smart meter data aggregation are build by using one of the following components or a combination of those. Some short examples of actual protocols will be given for each component, before in section 4 two protocols are discussed in detail.

3.1   Trusted third party

One simple approach to gain privacy through the aggregation of multiple smart meter data is presented in [2] and uses a trusted third party, the so called "aggregator". The aggregator is not part of any electricity provider and both the consumers as well as the providers rely on the trustworthiness of it: The consumers grant the aggregator access to their fine granulated smart meter data while the provider has only access to this aggregated results and therefore relies on the correct computation of these by the aggregator. As the electricity provider does not have access to individual smart meter data, this process ensures privacy if there is enough data combined in the aggregated result and the aggregator does not leak any other information. The drawback of this approach is that it just shifts the users necessary trust from the UC to the aggregator - however, as the aggregator does not have access to the UC's customer information, it might be more difficult for him to map a given smart meter to an exact household. The protocol explained in [13] also relies on third parties, however no entity in the protocol does get access to enough information to require any party to be fully trustworthy - two semi-trusted parties are sufficient here, as shown in section 4.2. Another drawback of these protocols is that the third party or parties each pose as a single point of failure.

The method shown in [4] can also be classified in this section, though it does not require one trustworthy aggregator but some trustworthy neighbours: Organized in a tree layout, each smart meter send its data in plaintext to its parent node in the tree through a short-range communication network. The parent sums all the data received by its child nodes and sends the aggregated data to its parent respectively. The utility company UC finally gets the data from the root node of this tree and therefore only receives the aggregated data of all smart meters in this neighbourhood. This method does not need any cryptography at all but the neighbours and everybody who's eavesdropping on the channel might be able to get individual smart meter data.

3.2   Secret sharing

A way to avoid the need for a trusted third party is to use secret sharing: In the protocol shown in [8], one smart meter splits its actual value v into multiple random chunks v_i so that $v = v_0 + \sum_{i=1}^{k} v_i$. Now, v_0 is kept private and each other v_i is encrypted with the public key of one of k other smart meters. Those k ciphertexts are then send to the UC. Once receiving all ciphertexts, the UC sends to each smart meter those ciphertexts, which are encrypted with his public key, so that each smart meter receives k encrypted chunks from k different smart meters. The smart meters then can decrypt those chunks, add their private v_0 and send the sum of all those plaintext chunks back to the UC. As every smart meter only receives a random part of another smart meters consumption, no smart meter learns any actual measurement data. Additionally, each of the sums, which the UC receives from the smart meters in plaintext, consists of random chunks from k different smart meters - so the UC does not get any information about the individual power consumption either. However, it can compute the total consumption of all k participants, which is good enough if those are all in the same geographical area.

The protocol is shown in figure 1, in which one also notices the obvious drawbacks of this method: Many different messages have to be sent and each of these has to be encrypted with the public key of another smart meter. This means an huge communication and computation overhead, and those resources are critical on devices like a smart meter. A way to minimize the necessary communication at the expense of an increased computation overhead is to also use homomorphic encryption (see section 3.4): In an additive homomorphic encryption scheme, the UC can sum encrypted data, without knowing the key needed for the decryption. So the UC then does not need to send k ciphertexts to each smart meter, but can sum the encrypted data and only send the encrypted sum to the smart meter for decryption.

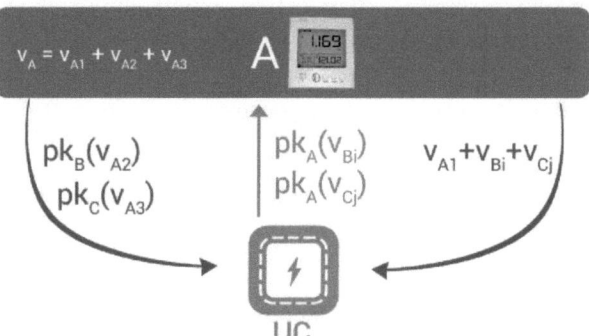

Fig. 1. Smart meter A splits its measurement in random chunks, each encrypted with the public key of another smart meter. After receiving ciphertexts from other smart meters, A can send the sum of those to the UC.

3.3   Masking

Another method used by several aggregation protocols is to mask the actual smart meter data with some random looking numbers. For the UC to still be able to get correct data, those random noises r_i, which are added to the data of each smart meter i have to be generated in a way to satisfy the equation $\sum_{i=1}^{k} r_i = 0$. This way, the UC can not trust the consumption reported by each individual smart meter but knows that the sum of all the received values is correct as the noise is eliminated in the aggregation.

Securely generating pseudorandom noise which sums to zero however is not trivial - if an eavesdropper or the UC is able to know r_i then he's able to unmask the data sent by smart meter i. Therefore, in [7] an additional trusted third party is required to generate and distribute those r_i to the appropriate smart meters. Some more sophisticated ways are presented in [10], for example a method based on the Diffie-Hellman key exchange protocol: Presume that each smart meter i has a private key sk_i and knows the public key $pk_j = g^{sk_j}$ of other participating smart meters, where g is the generator for a large cyclic group. g should be known to all participants, but should change every time the protocol is executed so that brute forcing the secret keys is not profitable. Now each smart meter i is able to calculate g^{r_i} with the following formula, where $j \prec i := \begin{cases} 1 \text{ if } j < i \\ 0 \text{ else} \end{cases}$:

$$ g^{r_i} = \prod_{j=1, j \neq i}^{k} pk_j^{(-1)^{j \prec i} \cdot sk_i} = \prod_{j=1, j \neq i}^{k} (g^{sk_j})^{(-1)^{j \prec i} \cdot sk_i} $$

This results in smart meter i generating a g^{r_i} for which r_i looks like the following:

$$ r_i = \sum_{j=1}^{i-1} -(sk_j \cdot sk_i) + \sum_{j=i+1}^{k} (sk_j \cdot sk_i) $$

So the sum $r = \sum r_i$ consists of $k \cdot (k-1)$ pairs of secret keys $(sk_i \cdot sk_j)$, while each of these pairs appears in a positive and a negative form once. Obviously, it is $r = 0$ then. Now as every smart meter has its mask g^{r_i} it can add its actual consumption data v by multiplying the mask with g^{v_i} and then send the number $g^{r_i + v_i}$ to the UC. The UC then multiplies all received data and thereby removes the masking effect of the r_i:

$$ \prod g^{r_i + v_i} = g^{\sum v_i + \sum r_i} = g^{\sum v_i} = g^{v_{total}} $$

As the problem of finding the discrete logarithm is NP-hard, [10] assumes that the UC roughly knows the approximated total consumption $\tilde{v}$ and then can brute force the actual consumption by comparing $g^{v_{total}}$ with $g^{\tilde{v}}, g^{\tilde{v}+1}, g^{\tilde{v}-1}, \dots$ until they match. This approach is depicted in figure 2.

A simpler approach to create the masking values at the cost of an increased communication effort is presented in [1] and [14]: Every smart meter generates a random data with each other smart meter in the neighbourhood by evaluating a pseudorandom function PRF. So instead of just needing to know the public key of the other smart meters like in the previous protocol, here every smart meter has to actually connect to all other smart meters and exchange the input seed for that PRF. Once two smart meters have generated such a random number together, one of them adds it to its actual value and the other one subtracts it. At the end of this exchange phase, every smart meter generated a sum of its measured value and $k - 1$ random numbers, which can then be send to the UC. The UC can easily eliminate the randomness by just summing all the data from the smart meters as each random value is added to one data and subtracted from another one.

These masking techniques still have some drawbacks though: First, there is still a high communication overhead to initially distribute all parameters (like the public keys or the seeds for the PRF) among the smart meters. These parameters should regularly change to avoid encrypting a lot of data with the same secrets. Also, if a new smart meter joins the network or disconnects from it, these parameters have to be negotiated again, as otherwise the property $\sum_{i=1}^{k} r_i = 0$ might not hold any more.

A second disadvantage when using masking is that the UC might be able to roughly estimate the real consumption at a given time by averaging data from several days: Independent of the distribution of these random noise values, the "central limit theorem" states that, given a sufficiently large number of samples, they will be normally distributed with an expected value μ. So by pointwise averaging the consumption of several days, chances are good we come close to the actual average consumption curve, vertically shifted by μ. However, due to the averaging, unusual peaks in the actual measurements are still hidden and the accuracy of the approximation is in general not good enough to identify active devices or other small characteristics.

3.4   Homomorphic encryption

By using a partial homomorphic encryption scheme, like the additive homomorphic Paillier scheme described in [12], one can apply an operation $\odot$ on two ciphertexts which then results in the application of another operation $\boxdot$ performed on the encrypted plaintext data, even if the key needed for decryption is unknown: $enc(m_1) \odot enc(m_2) = enc(m_1 \boxdot m_2)$. In the Paillier encryption scheme for example, multiplying two ciphertexts results in an addition of the encrypted data.

As smart meters have limited computing power, using homomorphic encryption might not seem like a good idea: Compared to other cryptosystems, it's generally a less efficient and more expensive method to encrypt data and produces larger ciphertexts. However, the advantages of homomorphic encryption for secure data aggregation are obvious and therefore it's used in many protocols. The method shown in [11] and pictured in figure 3 for example uses only a homomorphic encryption scheme: Organized in a binary tree structure, each smart meter encrypts its data with the public key of the UC, adds the encrypted data it receives from it's child nodes and sends the encrypted sum to the parent smart meter.

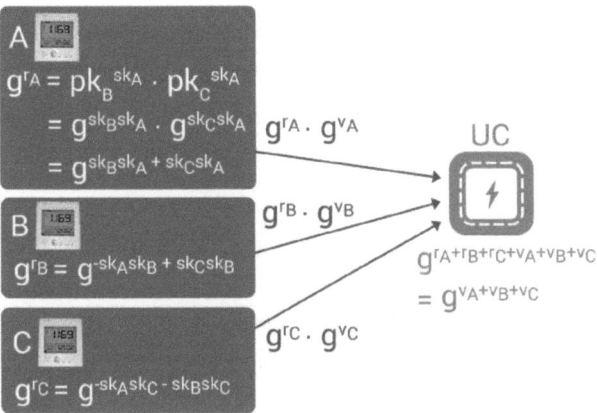

Fig. 2. The protocol proposed in [10] for generating masking data r out of the smart meters public keys $pk = g^{sk}$, so that $\sum r_i = 0$. The UC might be able to estimate the rough total value and use brute force to solve the discrete logarithm problem.

The root then sends the ciphertext of the sum of all the data to the UC which has the private key necessary for decrypting the sum. The protocol does not require much communication between the smart meters but does not provide any protection if the UC is able to eavesdrop on this communication: As each message is encrypted using only the UC's public key, the UC is able to decrypt every one of them.

In general, for the homomorphic property to work, all the involved ciphertexts have to encrypted with the same key. In [6] however, a slightly modified version of the homomorphic Paillier cryptosystem is used in combination with a secret sharing approach and allows each smart meter to use a different key: Instead of using the same public key $pk = (n, g)$ for the Paillier encryption, each smart meter i encrypts its data with a key (n_i, g) where the sum of all n_i equals n. What's special about this encryption scheme is that when multiplying all those ciphertexts, each encrypted with a different public key, one gets the sum of all the encrypted data in a form like it was encrypted using the public key $pk = (n, g)$. Every smart meter can act as an aggregator in this protocol, because the private key needed for decrypting the total sum is public - and this isn't a security issue as the decryption only works on the aggregated data. Another approach to use different keys and an homomorphic encryption scheme is used in [13] and will be explained in section 4.2 later.

Just like the secret sharing or the masking technique, using homomorphic encryption results in having to deal with some overhead: While there is no increase in the number of messages sent compared to the common direct reporting way, the message itself might be a lot bigger: For a key of length $n = 2048$ bit, the Paillier scheme will produce a 4096 bit long ciphertext - even if only a 32 bit integer has to be encrypted. Also, there is still a huge computational overhead for en- and decryption, even if just a partially homomorphic scheme like Paillier is used.

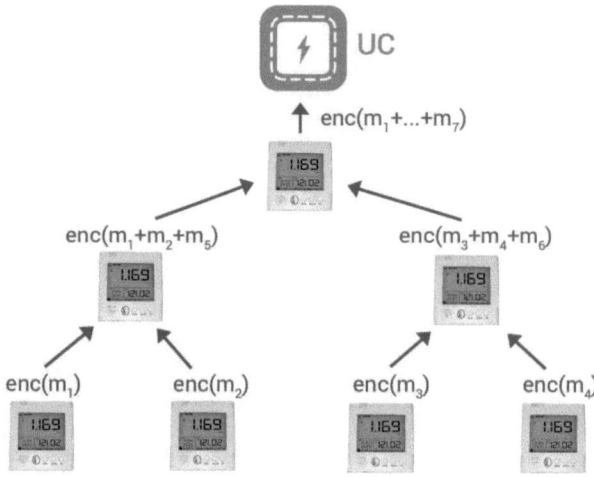

Fig. 3. By using a homomorphic encryption scheme, smart meters can sum up encrypted data without being able to decrypt it. The protocol fails if the UC is able to gain access to the messages sent between the smart meters.

4   Fault-tolerant and privacy-preserving data aggregation

For aggregation protocols, it is crucial that each participant of the protocol sends its data to the aggregation entity: On the one hand to ensure privacy (for example the homomorphic encryption based protocols do not add any protection if only one smart meter takes part in the protocol) and on the other to get correct results (protocols based on the masking technique for example require the data from all smart meters to correctly remove the masking). Some protocols don't work at all if only one communication link is broken: Imagine a round-robin protocol, where a smart meter receives data from one other, adds its own value and sends the data to the next one. This protocol will never deliver any data to the UC if the link between two smart meters is defective or if one smart meter is completely broken. As the smart meters in practice are placed in different households, connected through different ISP and, in some cases, even use a wireless communication network to connect to nearby smart meters, connection issues are very likely to occur. Many of the previously presented protocols do not consider this practical problem and assume a reliable network at all times. In this section, we will take a more detailed look at two modern proposals which address this issue.

4.1 Proactive fault-tolerant aggregation protocol

Won et al. described a fault-tolerant aggregation protocol in [14], which also considers smart meters dynamically joining and leaving the network. The protocol ensures ϵ-differential privacy for each household and also ensures differential privacy on the aggregated sum by adding gamma distributed noise to each measured value - as we will only focus on the aggregation aspect of the protocol, we will present a slightly simpler version without differential privacy statements on the total sum.

The protocol starts with a new smart meter i joining the network. At first, i has to randomly select k other smart meters as partner. As the protocol will aggregate the result of all these smart meters, one has to somehow make sure that all k partners are from within the same geographical region. As a load balancing method, each smart meter only accepts being the partner of at most $k + C$ other smart meters, where C is a predefined constant. If one smart meter refuses to be a partner, smart meter i randomly chooses a new one until k partners have accepted the partnership. Now, the new smart meter i negotiates a shared secret key with each of its k partners, for example by executing the Diffie-Hellman key exchange. Let $sk_{i,m}$ be the secret key, shared by smart meter i and m. When the smart meters report their measured data in time slot t, they first mask the information by adding the number $r_{i,t}$, where i marks the smart meter. $r_{i,t}$ is computed by evaluating different pseudo random number generators $PRNG$, each seeded with the shared secret key $sk_{i,j}$, at the position t. Be M the set of the k partners i chose and L the set of all smart meters, which chose i as their partner. Then $r_{i,t}$ is calculated using the following formula:

$$r_{i,t} = \sum_{j \in M} PRNG(sk_{i,j}, t) - \sum_{j \in L} PRNG(sk_{j,i}, t)$$

Let Ω be a closed set of smart meters, meaning that for each smart meter $i \in \Omega$ all k partners of i are also included in Ω, it is clear that $\sum_{i \in \Omega} r_{i,t} = 0$ for a fixed time slot t. So, as described in section 3.3, the UC is unable to get the measured data of an individual smart meter, but can get the aggregate sum of the power consumption of all smart meters in the closed set. So far, the protocol looks just like the one described in [1], however it is not yet fault tolerant: If a smart meter fails to report its masked data in a time slot t, then the masking data of the remaining smart meters will not sum up to zero and the UC is unable to get any useful information for t.

Therefore, the protocol also has a proactive mechanism to ensure fault tolerance: Instead of just sending the masked data for the current time slot, each smart meter also sends some data needed for unmasking future information. We assume the UC is able to store up to B messages per smart meter. The goal is now to always keep B entries per smart meter in this buffer: If there isn't any issue, each smart meter will transmit data for the current time slot t as well as some data for time slot $t + B$, which will be stored at the UC. So in time slot t, if the smart meter reports its data, the UC can use that and delete the previously transmitted and saved data for this slot. As it now only has $B - 1$ entries stored for that smart meter, it has enough space to also save the data transmitted for slot $t + B$. If a smart meter is unable to send data in t, it will try to send data for $t + 1, t + B$ and $t + B + 1$ in time slot $t + 1$ and the UC uses previously transmitted and saved data to unmask the other data in t. If it can't send data for two time slots, it will try to send the current and three future data in the next slot, and so on. This way, it takes $B + 1$ failed transmissions from a smart meter until the UC is unable to unmask any data.

In our simplified version of the protocol, data for the current time slot consists of the actual measured data and the generated masking number. Data for the future time slot $t + B$ has to contain $r_{i,t+B}$ as this number is needed to unmask the aggregated sum. However, if only this mask is transmitted, the UC would be able to get the individual measurement of smart meter i in time slot t by subtracting the future data sent in time slot $t - B$ from the current data. Therefore, a Laplace distributed random number $Lap(\lambda)$ is added to each future data. The described attack now does only give $m + Lap(\lambda)$, where m is the actual measurement. Depending on the noise scale λ, this still ensures ϵ-differential privacy. So if a smart meter is unable to send its data once, then the aggregated sum lacks the actual measurement of this smart meter and is distorted by $Lap(\lambda)$. However, the UC might be able to roughly estimate the missing measurement and a not perfectly accurate sum is still much better then not having any information about the consumption at all. According to [14], the error in their protocol is in $\mathcal{O}(\sqrt{w + 1})$ if w smart meters fail to report. A small scenario with two smart meters and a buffer with size $B = 3$ is shown in figure 4.

If a smart meter i keeps not sending any information or by choice want to leave the network, all of its k partners will have to generate new masking data and update all their future data in the UC's buffer. Also, those smart meters who chose i as their partner need to find a new one and generate new masks as well.

4.2 Multiparty computation under multiple keys

Another interesting, fault-tolerant protocol was introduced in 2013 by Peter et al. in [13]: Their approach uses two independent and not collaborating honest-but-curious servers S and C to compute the aggregated sum of the smart meters

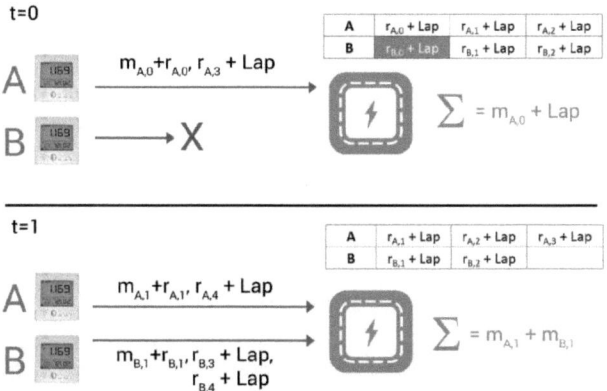

Fig. 4. Smart meter B fails to send its measurement in time slot $t = 0$: In the fault-tolerant protocol shown in [14], the UC uses its saved value to remove the masking in the aggregated result of the other smart meters and has to estimate B's consumption for that time slot. Note that A's actual data is still protected due to the added Laplacian noise. In $t + 1$, B has to send 2 future data sets to fill the buffer.

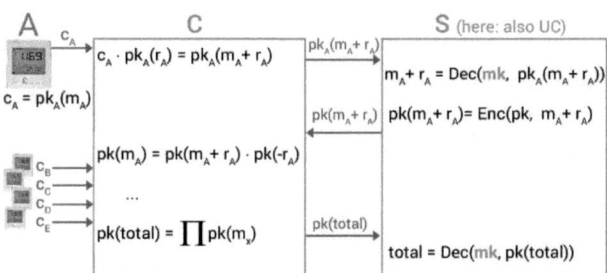

Fig. 5. The protocol presented in [13] with server S being the semi-trusted UC and C a semi-trusted third party. S has a master key mk to decrypt the smart meters ciphertexts, therefore C blinds the real values with r_A before sending it to S. S then transforms all the ciphertexts into an encryptions with the public key pk so C can make use of the homomorphic property and aggregate them.

data, while each smart meter uses a different key to encrypt its measurement. As neither S nor C will acquire enough information to know the consumption of a household, those servers don't have to be fully trusted - instead we just need them to not cooperate and share information between each other and therefore call them "semi-trusted" parties. The protocol uses the BCP encryption scheme, first presented in [3], in which encrypted data can be added by multiplying their corresponding ciphertexts. Before running the protocol, the server S has to generate the parameters needed for the BCP system and thereby obtains a "master key" mk. Then S publishes the public parameters, but keeps mk secret. The smart meters use the public BCP parameters to generate their public and private keys. As the BCP key generation algorithm is influenced by a random number, the keys of each smart meter will be random as well. The smart meters then encrypt their measurement using their own public key and the ciphertexts are uploaded to the second server C. The servers C and S now run a cryptographic protocol to calculate the sum of the encrypted data. Due to the homomorphic nature of the BCP scheme, calculating the encrypted sum without knowing the private key would be easy if all ciphertexts would have been encrypted under the same key pk. As this is not yet the case, C first needs to transform the ciphertexts into new ones, each then encrypted with a public key pk. In the protocol, pk is the product of all of the smart meters public keys. To transform a ciphertext, C adds a blinding value (which is easy as the smart meter's public key to encrypt the blinding is known and BCP is additively homomorphic so C can add two ciphertexts) and sends the blinded ciphertext to S. As S has the master key, it can decrypt any ciphertext without access to the private key of the any smart meter. So S decrypts the blinded measurement, encrypts it again with the new public key pk and sends the new ciphertext back to C. Again, C knows pk and therefore can subtract the previously added blinding number from the new ciphertext, resulting in the correct measurement now being encrypted with pk. In the process, neither C nor S can obtain the actual measurement: As C does not know the corresponding private key for pk, he is still not able to decrypt these ciphertexts. S on the other hand can decrypt any given ciphertext, but only got access to the masked data. After transforming all ciphertexts, C can calculated the aggregated sum on the new ciphertexts as they are now all encrypted using the same key pk. The result is again blinded, sent to S, encrypted and re-encrypted with the UC's public key, sent back to C to remove the blinding and then finally sent to the UC.

This approach will still be secure if C or S is the UC, like shown in figure 5 - however people might not trust the protocol if the UC has access to the master key. The other party can then for example be a governmental run server. Also, one has to make sure the communication between the smart meters and the server C is encrypted, as otherwise S is able break the security of the protocol by eavesdropping on this communication. Though not being highlighted in [13], the proposed protocol is - just like the trusted third party concept - fault-tolerant as it still works if some smart meters do not transmit data to the server C in a time slot. Those measurements are obviously not included in the aggregated sum then, so it might become a privacy issue if too many smart meters fail.

4.3 Comparison

There is no clear winner when comparing these two protocols: While both provide a fault-tolerant way to aggregate private smart meter data, their implementation is thereby the requirements are totally different. The proactive protocol described in 4.1 is basically an improved version of the masking concept and therefore is quite efficient once all parameters are set up. However, the UC is still able to roughly estimate consumption of a household by averaging multiple days and there is still a lot of peer-to-peer communication necessary to initially exchange all the shared secrets. Also, when a smart meter joins or leaves the network, lots of messages have to be send and many entries of the UC's buffer has to be invalidated, which results in additional overhead. Luckily, this should not happen too often and by just requiring one additional message with future data in each time slot, the protocol is nearly as efficient as the normal masking protocols.

Although using homomorphic encryption, the second protocol is also very efficient: There is no communication among the smart meters necessary and each smart meter only has to encrypt and send one message per time slot. However, this efficiency comes with a price: The protocol still requires two semi-trusted third parties. This is much better than the fully trusted third party approach, but still far from being ideal.

Both approaches are not as secure as the secret sharing protocol, but they seems to be a good trade-off between the necessary communication and computation overhead and the achieved privacy.

5   Conclusion

Several private aggregation techniques were shown in this work, however none of them is perfect yet: While the trusted third party approach is very efficient in terms of communication and computation overhead, one still has to trust another entity. Secret sharing is quite the opposite then: Nobody receives enough information to compute an individual consumption but this approach requires a lot of communication and encryption. Not quite as secure but more efficient are the masking protocols: The UC might be able to roughly average the individual consumption, but adding the masking data is a lightweight operation - only the distribution of the parameters among the smart meters requires some communication from time to time. Finally, using homomorphic encryption provides privacy - as long as the UC only acquires the encrypted total consumption - at the cost of an expensive encryption operation and an increased message size. Apart from the trusted third party protocol, for all these concepts it's crucial that all smart meters are reachable at all times. This is an impossible requirement in a real world deployment, so two fault-tolerant protocols have been presented in section 4: The first one is mainly based on masking - with all its pros and cons - and some additional Laplacian distributed random noise. The second one tries to combine several of the aggregation approaches to decrease the impact of their disadvantages: By using two semi-trusted parties, the protocol is as efficient and fault-tolerant as the trusted third party technique. However, by also using homomorphic encryption and masking, none of the two parties have to be fully trustworthy.

Though there are several pilot cities testing smart meters already, no information has been found on any aggregation protocol actually be implemented in one of those areas. One reason could be, that the tamper proof design of the smart meters prevents changes in its software and thereby a real world evaluation of the protocols. However, for many protocols the performance and other metrics have been analysed in simulations with real world data. And while none of the proposed protocols is absolutely perfect, in terms of privacy all of them are better then reporting the data from a single household directly to the utility company: The aggregation ensures privacy for all participants and the resulting data is still sufficient for the legitimate usage by the electricity provider. On the other hand, smart meter manufacturer and electricity companies do not really have any advantage in implementing those protocols as long as they are not legally required - and due to the tamper proof design of smart meters, the actual user does not have any influence on the software running on the meter in his household.

References

1. Acs, G., Castelluccia, C.: I have a dream! (differentially private smart metering). In: Filler, T., Pevny, T., Craver, S., Ker, A. (eds.) Information Hiding, Lecture Notes in Computer Science, vol. 6958, pp. 118–132. Springer Berlin Heidelberg (2011)
2. Bohli, J.M., Sorge, C., Ugus, O.: A privacy model for smart metering. In: Communications Workshops (ICC), 2010 IEEE International Conference on. pp. 1–5 (May 2010)
3. Bresson, E., Catalano, D., Pointcheval, D.: A simple public-key cryptosystem with a double trapdoor decryption mechanism and its applications. In: Laih, C.S. (ed.) Advances in Cryptology - ASIACRYPT 2003, Lecture Notes in Computer Science, vol. 2894, pp. 37–54. Springer Berlin Heidelberg (2003)
4. Choi, K., Chae, K.: Data aggregation using temporal and spatial correlations in advanced metering infrastructure. In: Information Networking (ICOIN), 2014 International Conference on. pp. 541–544 (Feb 2014)
5. Erkin, Z., Troncoso-Pastoriza, J., Lagendijk, R., Perez-Gonzalez, F.: Privacy-preserving data aggregation in smart metering systems: an overview. Signal Processing Magazine, IEEE 30(2), 75–86 (March 2013)
6. Erkin, Z., Tsudik, G.: Private computation of spatial and temporal power consumption with smart meters. In: Bao, F., Samarati, P., Zhou, J. (eds.) Applied Cryptography and Network Security, Lecture Notes in Computer Science, vol. 7341, pp. 561–577. Springer Berlin Heidelberg (2012)
7. Fan, C.I., Huang, S.Y., Lai, Y.L.: Privacy-enhanced data aggregation scheme against internal attackers in smart grid. Industrial Informatics, IEEE Transactions on 10(1), 666–675 (Feb 2014)
8. Garcia, F.D., Jacobs, B.: Privacy-friendly energy-metering via homomorphic encryption. In: Cuellar, J., Lopez, J., Barthe, G., Pretschner, A. (eds.) Security and Trust Management, Lecture Notes in Computer Science, vol. 6710, pp. 226–238. Springer Berlin Heidelberg (2011)
9. Greveler, U., Justus, B., Loehr, D.: Multimedia content identification through smart meter power usage profiles. Computers, Privacy and Data Protection (2012)
10. Kursawe, K., Danezis, G., Kohlweiss, M.: Privacy-friendly aggregation for the smart-grid. In: Fischer-Huebner, S., Hopper, N. (eds.) Privacy Enhancing Technologies, Lecture Notes in Computer Science, vol. 6794, pp. 175–191. Springer Berlin Heidelberg (2011)
11. Li, F., Luo, B., Liu, P.: Secure information aggregation for smart grids using homomorphic encryption. In: Smart Grid Communications (SmartGridComm), 2010 First IEEE International Conference on. pp. 327–332 (Oct 2010)
12. Paillier, P.: Public-key cryptosystems based on composite degree residuosity classes. In: Stern, J. (ed.) Advances in Cryptology EUROCRYPT 99, Lecture Notes in Computer Science, vol. 1592, pp. 223–238. Springer Berlin Heidelberg (1999)
13. Peter, A., Tews, E., Katzenbeisser, S.: Efficiently outsourcing multiparty computation under multiple keys. Information Forensics and Security, IEEE Transactions on 8(12), 2046–2058 (Dec 2013)
14. Won, J., Ma, C.Y., Yau, D.K., Rao, N.S.: Proactive fault-tolerant aggregation protocol for privacy-assured smart metering. In: The 33rd Annual IEEE International Conference on Computer Communications (2014)

All images in the text are made by the author